Discover Real Happiness

CHAPTER ONE

UNDERSTANDING HAPPINESS

WE SPEND MOST OF OUR lives searching for happiness—the elusive quality that will make everything right once we manage to capture it. Happiness *can* be achieved but only if you know and understand *what* happiness is. Once you know this, you will be able to focus on what it is that makes you happy.

Our requirements for happiness, and our interpretation of its meaning, change at various stages during our lives. As teenagers, happiness is the latest fashion, music, or craze. As we get older, happiness might mean falling in love for the first time, buying a car, owning our own home, starting a family. "Happiness or Gratification?" on pages 18-19 highlights the distinction between what you might want in the short-term and what will give you longer-lasting pleasure.

We spend much of our time fretting over practical and financial matters, often believing that a windfall is all it would take to make us happy. The research about wealth and happiness cited on pages 22-23 shows that those who have great wealth are not significantly happier than the rest of us, and that although financial security is important, it is not as important to our happiness as being able to have satisfying relationships with others.

Work, too, ranks as a very important part of our lives and often has a tremendous influence on our happiness and peace of mind. Working can give us a sense of worth and value and provide an important opportunity for interacting with others. In "A Working Life?" on pages 26-27, we look at the elements that contribute toward a fulfilled professional life and suggest strategies for achieving more satisfaction in your job.

But in order to get to grips with what happiness is, it helps to know how happiness works for other people. In "Happy People" and "Traits of Happy People" (see pp. 28-31) we take a close look at what makes a happy person and identify the sources of this happiness. We find that it has little to do with external factors but a lot to do with a positive mindset. Happy people have identifiable traits that you can adopt so that you, too, can achieve happiness.

Being happy is a decision we can all make in our lives. Concentrating on living in the present and leaving past regrets behind can be a liberating experience. "Decide to Be Happy," pages 36-37, provides a formula for happiness that you can use as a guide to identifying and incorporating happiness into your life.

HAPPINESS IS WITHIN YOUR REACH HERE, NOW, IN THE PRESENT, NOT IN THE PAST OR IN THE FUTURE. SO OPEN UP YOUR MIND TO THE POSSIBILITY OF BEING HAPPY—TODAY!

LEARNING TO BE HAPPY

H OW DO WE LEARN about happiness, or rather how do we acquire the mental well-being that enables us to experience happiness? Child specialist Dr. D. W. Winnicott once said, "You cannot teach a child to be happy," and some psychologists do argue that in terms of temperament, the dye is cast at conception. However, childhood influences, environmental factors, and life events also shape our view of ourselves and life in general—positive and negative.

Growing up

Looking at the research on happiness for clues, we discover that self-esteem and a personal sense of control are commonly found in happy people—they know and value who they are, and have a good idea of what works for them.

The way we evolve a view of ourselves has much to do with the way we are treated by others, and what we think and feel about that treatment. From birth, other people's reactions to us are paramount. Small children constantly watch the adults around them, learning by example and drawing on their reactions to make sense of the world. If a child feels he or she is being treated with respect, this helps to develop and enhance feelings of self-worth. In the same way, if children are encouraged to discover for themselves what they like to do, they will evolve their own ideas of what is satisfying, and find their own recipe for happiness. But if a child is led to believe he or she is stupid, or in the way, this becomes a breeding ground for feelings of unworthiness and insecurity.

It's never too late

However, there is plenty of evidence that it's never too late to change and grow. The American psychologist E. R. Guthrie cites the case of a plain female student

who became the butt of a college prank when a number of male classmates decided to treat her as if she were the most popular girl in class and all asked her out for a date. After a number of dates, something unexpected took place. Her bogus beaus began to find her genuinely attractive, and the girl began to see herself in a new, more positive light, an assumption that grew stronger as time went by.

This case study demonstrates that what we tell ourselves is very powerful in determining self-worth and self-esteem. If the girl had told herself all along that she was attractive, and worthy of attention, she would have behaved as such. No matter what we have been told before, good or bad, we need to be aware of the way we perceive ourselves, for it is this that forms the basis of our happiness.

___

A picture of reflections
We put together a picture of ourselves,
based on the way other people treat us
and appear to perceive us.
___

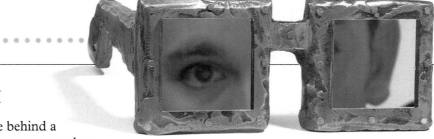

CHANGING

It's not easy to leave behind a childhood of negative messages, but it is possible. While it may feel scary to start to believe something new about yourself, you can do it. If you find yourself thinking negatively, remind yourself that that was then and this is now and you are choosing to do things differently. See the exercise as an exciting adventure. Of course, things won't change overnight, but if you stick at it, you will find your self-image becoming more and more positive. The following points will help you to do this:

• Build a new picture of yourself. Gather as much evidence of your positive attributes as you can: you're kind, generous, attentive. Remember, too, the skills you have: "I'm good at playing the piano," "I'm a whizz at computers," "I'm a fantastic cook," "I'm good with figures." Say them out loud and write them down. "Own" them. Include all your achievements, everything from "I was awarded a junior swimming medal for swimming the length of the local pool," to "I gained a hard-earned professional qualification."

• Ask for positive statements from your most trusted friends. It is vital that you hear from others just how much you are valued.
• Keep a journal in which you write down all the good things that happen, all the positive things people say to you—try to absorb these vital influences at the time and then reinforce them by reading through the journal now and again as a reminder of your positive self-image.
• Start to recognize negative self-statements. Ask yourself where they came from. Are they true? What do you want to do differently?
• When you start to feel low, ask yourself what you can do to avoid such feelings becoming entrenched. Do you need time alone, or would spending time with others lift your mood?
• Not all negative feelings stem from within. If your outer circumstances are contributing to your low spirits, look at practical ways in which you can improve matters.

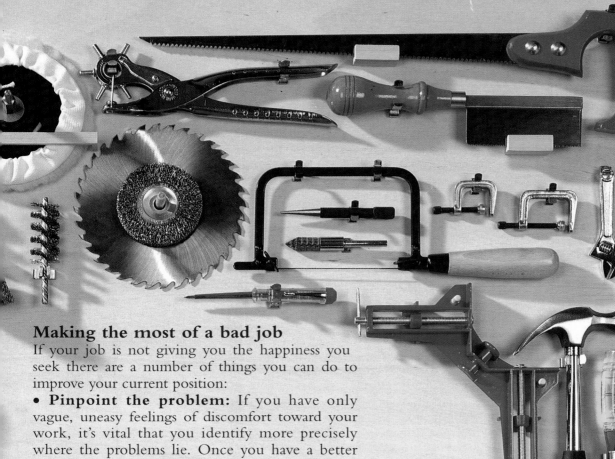

Making the most of a bad job

If your job is not giving you the happiness you seek there are a number of things you can do to improve your current position:

• **Pinpoint the problem:** If you have only vague, uneasy feelings of discomfort toward your work, it's vital that you identify more precisely where the problems lie. Once you have a better understanding of your difficulties, you can devise a strategy to overcome them.

• **Change your approach or attitude:** Improve your time-management skills, for example, by reading up on the subject or taking a course. Or brush up on your interpersonal skills. Cultivate a more positive attitude toward your work, and you may find others respond in kind.

• **Work in harmony with yourself:** Most people are either larks or owls. Larks are bright and alert first thing in the morning, owls tend to get going as the day wears on. Try to reschedule the sort of work you tackle to suit your natural rhythm—if you're a lark, work on mentally demanding tasks early in the day; if you're an owl, leave it until midday to exercise your cognitive skills. This may make all the difference to how you perform at work and the way you feel about your job.

Getting things into perspective

You may, of course, come to the conclusion that seeking a new position is your only option. This is rarely an instant solution; it takes time and effort to find a new job that meets most of your requirements. In the meantime, do everything you

Tools of the trade
A degree of happiness at work is possible for everyone, no matter what they do or how much they earn.

can to improve your present circumstances, as described above. In particular, make very sure that the problem is the job, and not you, otherwise you will simply take your troubles with you to your next position.

For many of us, work plays a central role in our lives, so it's vital that you find the right job profile for you. But you also need time for your family and leisure interests. Make it a priority to find a balance between these two important parts of your life—to appreciate what each contributes in its different way.

HAPPY PEOPLE

I S HAPPINESS DUE TO A mysterious, undiscovered gene? You might well believe so, since some people appear to enjoy life without effort, while others feel that their attempts to achieve happiness have been thwarted by painful circumstances. Research has indicated that, while a person's capacity for happiness can be predicted by his or her personality traits, this same capacity can be enhanced, with a little effort, by studying and understanding the traits of happy people.

Several studies suggest that happy people tend to view the world optimistically. Even if their perspective is frequently derided as viewing life through "rose-colored spectacles," it nonetheless provides the inspiration needed to transcend daily hassle or hardship. People who are less happy, by contrast, interpret life's difficulties in an unduly negative and pessimistic way. The psychologist M. W. Eysenck suggests that unhappy people wear "blue-colored spectacles"; for them, happiness is seen as "transitory and undeserved." Find out the color of your spectacles—or make the decision to change them—by discovering whether you have most of the significant traits of happy people.

3. Happy people are full of hope

Despite its hardships, life is seen by happy people as a journey or even an adventure worth a few risks. Their optimism and resilience is tempered by discrimination and a realistic appraisal of life—very often learned from their mistakes! Happy people are often curious, flexible, and creative in their approach to life.

2. Happy people believe they have some control over life

Achieving and doing something well, especially against the odds, can be a great source of pride and self-respect. Psychologists describe a faith in one's abilities and judgment as an "internal locus of control." Happy people tend to establish their own goals and actively set out to achieve them.

1. Happy people have self-esteem

The best predictor of happiness is satisfaction with self. People who know and accept themselves enjoy life, trust their judgment, do not dwell on mistakes or failures, and pursue their goals despite difficulties. Because they have faith in themselves, they are usually able to initiate and sustain relationships, and focus on their good points rather than failings.

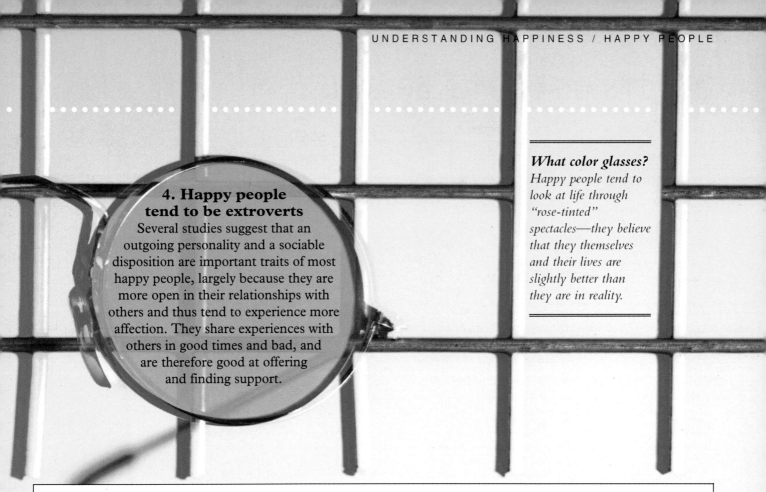

4. Happy people tend to be extroverts

Several studies suggest that an outgoing personality and a sociable disposition are important traits of most happy people, largely because they are more open in their relationships with others and thus tend to experience more affection. They share experiences with others in good times and bad, and are therefore good at offering and finding support.

What color glasses?
Happy people tend to look at life through "rose-tinted" spectacles—they believe that they themselves and their lives are slightly better than they are in reality.

WHO'S HAPPY?

Because appearing happy is a socially desirable trait, many people often feel compelled to say they're happy when they're not. So how can you recognize happiness in others? Of course, not all happy people will demonstrate the following traits all of the time, but they are a fair indication of a person's state of mind.

Facial expression

Most happy people smile often, although smiling can be a way to cloak real feelings. The spontaneous smile usually affects the upper part of the face: the cheeks rise, crinkling the eyes so that they appear smaller.

Posture

Happy people tend to maintain an upright position whether they are sitting or standing. Their chests are not covered by their arms, their shoulders are back, they breathe easily, and they move with confidence.

Eye movement

People who are glad to see you look into your eyes and maintain eye contact. A steady, gentle gaze very often signals happiness, and shining eyes usually indicate vitality and joy.

Tone of voice

The tone of our voice is probably our most spontaneous tool of communication, so this can be a reliable indicator of mood. People who are trying to appear happy, but speak in a dull voice, are probably not truly cheerful.

Crying out for help

Martin seemed to get involved in minor car crashes on a very regular basis, and suffered frequent sporting accidents playing amateur football. However, what was really happening was that Martin was unconsciously expressing his need for help and compassion through self-destructive behavior.

Attention seeking

Clare was late for everything. Her family would sit waiting in the car with the engine running while Clare repainted her finger nails or changed her outfit—anything to keep them waiting. Tempers would flare, but Clare's need for attention was greater than the negative reaction she caused.

person. Such behavior, which is usually unconscious, is known as secondary gain. Because it involves using yourself as a manipulative tool to get at, or to, someone else, it may well conflict with your desire to feel happy, and may lead you to sacrifice your own happiness in order to fulfill a deeper need. For some people this means "winning" by losing, as this secures either attention and concern from others, or affords them, they believe, a safe way of expressing anger at authority figures (see box, left). The problem with secondary gain is that more often than not it doesn't work, and leaves those you're trying to "get at" completely unaware of what you are doing and so incapable of responding in the way you would wish them to.

Uncovering your motives

Secondary gain is usually deeply unconscious and can take time to uncover: None of us likes to admit that we're behaving in a destructive way, expressing those damaged parts of ourselves that we find too painful to address in a more direct manner. The only thing we may be aware of is the deep unhappiness and dissatisfaction we feel toward ourselves and our lives. While professional help is usually needed to unravel the problem, it may be possible to uncover your own need for secondary gain by asking yourself if there is any way that you might be gaining through failing. With whom might you be angry? Who might you want to affect in order to get a response of concern and attention?

Stop the sabotage

Trying to stop this damaging behavior pattern isn't something that can be achieved overnight, as your reasons for not wanting to be happy or fulfilled may be very complex. However, as a first step, try asking yourself what it is you might gain by not being happy. Try to become aware of how and when and why you feel guilty; for example, whose voice do you hear telling you that you don't deserve happiness? Ask yourself why you might feel that others have failed you.

By identifying the reasons for your behavior, acknowledging them, and then attempting to modify or stop your need to sabotage, you might also discover an even deeper emotion: a feeling that you do, in fact, deserve to be happy.

TOO GOOD TO LAST?

Why would anyone be afraid of love and happiness? However impossible this seems, the truth is that few people explore their full potential for joy because they suspect happiness is "too good to last." In the context of personal relationships, fear of happiness often goes hand in hand with fear of rejection; it is safer, people reason, to avoid intimacy rather than face the pain of a broken relationship. This view may include new friendships, which also require energy and commitment.

Under certain circumstances, fear is a healthy self-protective emotion, for example when dealing with danger. In its mildest form it is experienced as excitement, which is why thrillers and daring feats make such popular entertainment. Most actors will tell you that without a *frisson* of stage fright their performance will lack charisma. And both fear and falling in love produce surges of adrenalin, which feel like a rush of energy. But it is when fear becomes a way of life, or a self-defeating way of behaving, that it cripples our potential and diminishes our potential for happiness.

Learning to change

Since fear, like anger, is part of our emotional make-up, there is little point in trying to suppress or deny it. Psychologists stress acceptance and understanding as the first steps on the road to developing new behavior patterns and ways of thinking. Until you become aware of your reactions, you will behave as you have always done. This behavior is greatly influenced by the relationships you experienced with adults when you were a child, when your beliefs about love and relationships were first formed. Looking at your personal history will help you understand and expose your fears. You can then work toward change by taking responsibility for yourself and choosing to create a happier life, rather than remain a powerless victim. You can explore these areas with the aid of one of the many self-help books available, with tapes, or by working with a trained counselor.

Lonely hearts

Many peoples' fears about closeness represent an agreement they have made with themselves that, inevitably, contains a faulty conclusion. For example, if you never try to get to know someone better, you will never have to face the pain of being rejected. On the one hand this statement is true. On the other, the results produced by this conclusion are painful.

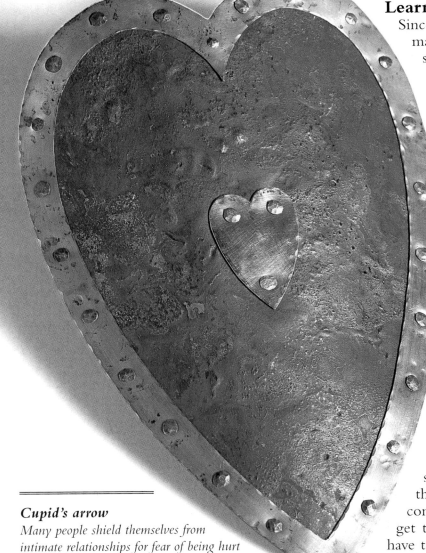

Cupid's arrow
Many people shield themselves from intimate relationships for fear of being hurt or disappointed.

Having no intimate relationships, either with friends or sexual partners, creates intense feelings of loneliness and rejection, exactly what the faulty conclusion was designed to protect you from. This cruel paradox must be faced before we can do anything about allowing more love into our lives. The key to all this is self-love—or self-esteem—coupled with self-awareness.

Think positive

Once you have identified the thoughts, beliefs, and actions associated with your fear, you can begin to replace them with different, more positive ones. This process can be exhilarating, so don't allow fear to build up, or think that you can never change your life. First, ask yourself some questions:

• If part of you does want a relationship, what part of you does not?

• Are you afraid of being trapped?

• Are you afraid of intimacy or getting too close?

• Do you feel that you are unlovable?

• Are your expectations unrealistic?

• Is your vision of a relationship rigid and limited to just one specific type of person? Or do you have too vague an idea of what you are looking for?

Many experts recommend acting "as if" you already have what you desire. Being receptive, excited by life, and experiencing joyful feelings are all characteristics of someone in love. But these characteristics can also be evoked in other ways: give yourself some little treat, such as buying a bunch of flowers or a lovely meal, on a regular basis. Treasure your existing friendships, and don't regard them as a way to mark time until your "significant other" arrives. Above all, love yourself— good and bad traits alike. As you begin to release your fears and value yourself more highly, so you will attract others who value you, too.

CHOOSING TO CHANGE

If you are afraid of relationships, do not blame yourself, your parents, or other people in your life. It is acceptance and self-knowledge that will turn you from a victim of fate into a powerful person who is in charge of your life and your relationships. It really is not very difficult. For example, if you dislike pickles, you don't eat them, you choose to avoid them. In the same way, you can choose to avoid self-defeat and limitations. Here are some pointers for facilitating this type of change:

• Get a notebook and write down your thoughts about relationships. Some will be negative: "People always let me down," and some positive: "I would like to have more friends."

• Then, as many experts recommend, turn these statements into affirmations that you can repeat to yourself. Write them on cards placed where you will see them, or write them out at least ten times each day until they become part of you and your new beliefs. If, for example, you believe, "People always let me down," you might replace this with an affirmation such as: "I am now attracting supportive, loving people into my life." If you would like more friends, you could affirm this wish in a similar way.

• Creative visualization (see pp. 78-79) is another helpful technique. Try imagining a fulfilling relationship or exciting social life. How does it feel? What does it include? Be as specific as you can. What can you do to develop yourself so that you are more in tune with this inner picture?

It is important to support affirmations and all other inner work with actions. If you want to expand your personal life, you might join a class, sports club, or do voluntary work. Taking action shows your subconscious mind that you mean business. The very simple act of deciding to tackle your fears means that you have already created inner change. Everything else will follow.

of your happiness. If you are locked into a world of resentment, anger, and disappointment you may miss the good things that will happen to you along the way. You may also believe that you should never admit to yourself or anyone else when you do feel unhappy. But not letting yourself feel disappointed or hurt forces away other valuable emotions and experiences that may enrich your life or your relationships, such as love, concern, care, desire, and passion. To maintain a healthy balance, it is important to know when to address your painful feelings and when to be open to what is pleasurable.

Light and shade

Living in a state of constant happiness would be like living exposed to permanent brightness. It is, in fact, much more interesting to take a path that leads us through both light and shade, so that we can appreciate the warmth and brightness of the sun, as well as the gentle cool of the shadows.

REALISTIC EXPECTATIONS

A common obstacle to happiness is unrealistic expectations—it's no good wanting to be a doctor if you've never been good at science. Similarly, if you go to every party anticipating the social event of the year, or expect your vacations to be two weeks of bliss, you may be setting yourself up for a disappointment. To find happiness your expectations must be realistic and achievable within the context of your life and abilities.

The cold light of day

There's nothing wrong with dreaming—most achievements, creative, technical, or otherwise, would not have come about if they hadn't started with someone having a powerful dream, or an inspired "What if?" On a day-to-day level, we've all enjoyed daydreaming and make-believe—pursuits of this sort can be an imaginative source of ideas that may turn into something more concrete.

But dreams can be destructive, too. Take the example of the vacation mentioned above. Imagine that it's a family get-together that includes a range of generations. It's normal to anticipate an ostensibly enjoyable activity with pleasure—that's human nature. But pinning unrealistic hopes on it can be more devastating than if you'd worked out beforehand where some of the problems might lie—that grandma is fussy about her food and you need to cater specially for her, or that with children in your party you need to choose an area where there is a range of things to do that are geared toward them.

Stars in your eyes?
Dreams are a vital source of inspiration, but unless you dream with your feet firmly on the ground your dreams can be shattered by unrealistic expectations.

There is a difference between daydreams and an inspiring vision, and between idle thoughts and a deeply felt aspiration. Understanding what the difference is is vital. Never to raise your eyes to the stars is to miss out on passion, vision, and grace; but if you are always looking upward you run the risk of tripping over and hurting yourself.

Why do we dream?

The most destructive daydreams are those we use to escape from a painful reality. Such dreams only compound the problem by contributing to our feelings of discontent with reality. For a number of people, there is strong hope attached to a dream—perhaps they'll win the lottery and then their lives will be different, or they'll lose lots of weight overnight and have an ideal figure. These dreams are, in the main, unrealistic. Without a clear sense of purpose, and a sound strategy to implement and support the dream (see box, right), the person is prevented from addressing the real issues of his or her life.

We all need to know where to draw the line between fact and fiction. It may be painful to face reality, but the alternative can have serious repercussions. If you feel your dream getting out of control, you will need to rein yourself in and review your dreams. How realistic are they? Ask yourself, "What do I hope to gain by pursuing this dream?" Try to analyze what lies behind your fantasies—perhaps it is something you really want, perhaps not.

A STRATEGY FOR SUCCESS

Self-styled leadership guru Anthony Robbins has devoted an entire book, *Unlimited Power*, to how to go about realizing your dreams. His message is dare to dream, but understand at the same time that dreams don't get accomplished of their own accord; you need to act on your dreams if you want results. Certain characteristics need to be in place, including a passion for your dream, belief that you can make it happen, and a strategy to make it come about. Robbins also cites getting your values clear, having the energy to make your dream happen, and communicating well with others. Robbins argues that there are four steps to success, which he calls the "Ultimate Success Formula." These are:

Matching your dreams to reality

Not all dreams have to be turned into workable strategies as suggested in the box, right, nor do they have to be put behind you. By all means day-dream, but be clear that this is what you are doing. Some people turn their dreams into a hobby or interest. Frances, for example, fantasized about being a ballroom dancer. The fact that she didn't have the figure—or talent—of a professional dancer didn't stop her from dreaming. Then she saw a local ad for beginners' ballroom classes. Harry, her husband, agreed to go to the classes with her, and they both thoroughly enjoyed themselves. Frances accepted that her dream was never going to turn into a career, but the classes gave both of them a great deal of pleasure.

1. Know what you want: Set yourself a definite goal.

2. Take action: Form a plan, broken up into stages, to take you to your goal. Do you have the skills you need? Do you need to retrain? Set your plan in motion.

3. Watch your progress: Monitor whether your actions are taking you closer to your goal, and learn from your experiences.

4. Be flexible: Develop the flexibility to change your behavior until you get what you want. If one course of action isn't working, try another...and another. Successful people are not afraid to change tack, so be open to trying things differently if necessary.

CHAPTER THREE

PERSONAL FULFILLMENT

OUR HAPPINESS IS VERY dependent on whether or not we feel personally fulfilled. If we do not, we will experience regret, disappointment, and, possibly, anger. But when we do achieve fulfillment, there is a glow of satisfaction and happiness that makes us feel more alive.

Personal fulfillment can only be achieved if you have an identifiable dream or aspiration. "Follow Your Dreams," pages 74-75, explains that we all have the chance to change—either ourselves or our lives—but in order to do this, you have first to define your goals. Knowing what you want is the first step toward happiness and inner contentment, and "Getting What You Want," pages 76-77, deals with the problem of trying to make your goals a reality. Practical help toward achieving this is given on pages 78-79, "It's All in the Mind," which explains how an extremely effective method of mind training known as creative rehearsal can be harnessed so that you can achieve your particular goal and find true satisfaction.

A large part of attaining personal fulfillment is getting the balance right in your life. Doing things because you have to, or because you are expected to, may mean that you are not doing enough for *you*, and subsequently not fulfilling your potential. "Are You Getting the Balance Right?" pages 80-81, takes a look at this problem and, with the help of a quiz, will enable you to identify problem areas and how to redress them. Many of us are guilty of allowing various elements in our lives to take over, and of putting our own needs in second place to those of others. On pages 82-83, "Maintaining Your Balance," we look at the importance of balancing your personal needs with other social and work commitments.

But how can you be personally fulfilled if you're trying to be something you're not? "Accepting Yourself" (see pp. 84-85) stresses that you should not become what others want you to be— you should be who you are. Although it is important to be flexible in your dealings with others, it is even more important to remain true to yourself and have the courage to stick to your beliefs.

Finally, "Appreciate Your Happiness," pages 90-91, stresses the importance of not undervaluing what you already have. By concentrating on what you do not have and always striving for more, you may miss the undoubted riches you already possess.

TO ACHIEVE PERSONAL FULFILLMENT, YOU MUST BE PREPARED TO TAKE ACTION TOWARD YOUR GOAL. WHEN YOU DO, YOU WILL FIND THAT ALL SORTS OF EXTRAORDINARY THINGS MAY BEGIN TO HAPPEN.

What's Important to You?

YOU MAY THINK you know yourself inside out, but do you? You may find on closer examination that this belief is based on a false image you have of yourself. If, for example, you decide early on that you are someone who needs his or her creature comforts—and lots of them—you may be overlooking an even stronger need for close relationships, or substituting one for the other.

This quiz will help you to think about yourself in terms of your inner priorities. You may be surprised by your responses, or they may confirm what you already know about yourself. Think carefully about each of the statements below, choosing **a**, **b**, **c**, or **d**. Add up your scores, and turn to page 138 for an analysis of your responses.

1. You are shipwrecked on a beautiful desert island. What would you most want to discover there:
a) A chest full of valuable treasure?
b) That your partner, family, or a close friend had been shipwrecked there too?
c) A battery-operated two-way radio so that you could keep in touch with the outside world while you await rescue?
d) A supply of something that gives you great pleasure, such as a collection of good books, or a music system and CDs?

2. Doctors have told you you've got a year to live. You're in good health at the moment and can do anything you want. Would you:
a) Take every last cent you have out of the bank and buy all the objects you have ever longed to possess?
b) Spend as much time as you could with the people you really care about?
c) Determine to use this time to make a real mark at work, or to achieve something you have dreamed of professionally?
d) Give up work and have as much fun as possible, traveling and doing all the things you've always wanted to do?

3. You're given a magic wand that can change one thing in your life. Would it be:
a) To win the lottery?
b) To have more fulfilling relationships?
c) To be offered the most prestigious position that you could hold in your field of work?
d) To be young again, carefree, and not to have any responsibilities or ties?

Look into yourself
It is only through very close self-examination that you will become aware of your innermost needs and wants.

4. You're offered a very desirable position at work, but there is one hitch. The hitch is one of the reasons below. Would you turn down the job because:
a) Although the work is very interesting and responsible, the pay is not good?
b) The greater responsibility will inevitably mean your family and social life will suffer?
c) It is a distraction from your long-term career strategy?
d) Your new position will put you in a more formal position with your work colleagues?

5. A friend, a mature student who has taken up an art course, has invited you to her year-end exhibition at the local college. Do you:
a) Sound non-commital—student art doesn't particularly appeal to you?
b) Make every effort to see her show?
c) Tell her you can't go—the exhibition is open only during the day in the week, and it would interfere with work?
d) Tell her you'll try to go, keeping your options open in case something more interesting comes up?

6. You are looking for a new place to live. Do you:
a) Look for the most expensive, prestigous apartment you can afford in the "right" area?
b) Try to find somewhere that's close to friends and family?
c) Make it a priority to search out properties within a certain traveling distance of your place of work?
d) Look for a neighborhood that's full of life and interest—bars, restaurants, a cinema, that kind of thing?

7. When you're planning a vacation, do you:
a) Go for the most glamorous location you can afford?
b) Make every effort to include family or friends?
c) Consider your work commitments first—as far as you are concerned, the job comes before vacations?
d) Focus on locations that offer you the scope to engage in your favorite pursuits?

8. In which one way do you wish you had lived your life differently? Do you:
a) Wish you had had more money to enable you to have had a higher standard of living?
b) Wish you had handled your relationships with your partner/friends or family better?
c) Wish you had chosen a totally different career?
d) Wish you had allowed more time for your interests and the things you enjoy doing?

The right mix
Happiness is about mixing the different elements of your life in the right proportions.

Home	Hours	Rating
• shopping		
• preparing food and eating		
• housework: cleaning, etc.		
With partner/spouse		
• talking, discussing, arguing		
• relaxing		
• sharing an activity		
• making love, cuddling, being affectionate		
Alone		
• relaxing at home		
• hobbies, part-time courses		
• doing nothing, daydreaming		
• physical activities, exercise		
• sleeping		

Maintaining Your Balance

Like the forces of nature, we, too, strive to maintain a balance in our lives in the face of conflicting demands or emotions. Very often, however, we find a balance that feels "normal," but which is in fact unhealthy and may be working against our needs. An extreme example of this is addictive behavior: satisfying the need feels necessary in order to create a stable state, but in fact the addiction is also damaging the body. A less extreme case is that of the executive who works long hours in order to pay for a certain lifestyle, but ignores the fact that as a result relationships with friends and family are out of kilter.

What is balance?

In an age when most of us are having to juggle work, family, and other demands, getting the balance right can seem an impossible goal. You may feel satisfied at the end of the day that you've managed to do almost everything you planned to do, but this has nothing to do with real balance, and you may be devoting more time to trying to meet the needs of others, rather than your own.

Bobbing along

Many of us spend our lives leaning too far in one direction, and then too far in the other. True balance is harder, but not impossible, to achieve.

For some people, recreation is also a problem. At its worst, free time becomes non-time, a period when we slip into a state of joyless apathy, and we are incapable of creatively or fulfillingly using our leisure hours. In addition, many of us labor at having fun, as well as working hard during the day—making every day and evening a highly pressured existence. Living this way means our minds and bodies aren't allowed simply to "be," as they are continuously called upon to perform and "do."

True balance is about being in tune with your inner needs and responding appropriately to them. It is vitally important that your need for activity and tension is on a parallel with your need for relaxation and pleasure—to achieve equilibrium, activity must be counter-balanced with passivity. Sharing these elements in a way that makes you happy and fulfilled is what balance is all about.

Find your "tuning fork"

Life is a constant round of change and stress, so it's essential that you find your own way of reviving your inner energy and harmony. Balance is like a sixth sense: it doesn't come from outside, it is something you have to find within yourself. If you're truly balanced, then you will automatically, without being conscious of it, be in harmony with your inner "tuning fork." When the tone of your life feels too high or too low, you will instantly adjust, naturally and with ease. This is a skill that

we're not born with, but one that must be acquired, often through trial and error, like learning how to ride a bike or a becoming a swimmer, over a period of time.

Individual needs

The difficulty with finding a balance is that each of us is different—our needs are unique and our tuning forks are individually created. Most of us know that the single most effective way of achieving a balance in an otherwise busy life is to relax, but how we achieve this varies according to the individual: You might create a balance by listening to music, your friend might play a sport, while another friend prefers time alone.

To get the best from your life you must give equal effort to the different strands of it, typically work, home, and play. Satisfaction at work, for example, will enhance personal relationships and social life. Similarly, a stable and loving home life will have a positive effect on work. Although the balance will be different for different people, the journey of discovery will be the same. Whatever it takes for you to find a balance in your life, do it.

KEEPING ON AN EVEN KEEL

Balance is all about allowing the various elements in your life to occupy only as much time and attention as they require in order to fulfill you. To achieve this degree of satisfaction with your work and personal life, consider the following:

• Identify what is tipping the balance unfavorably. One reason why we get out of balance is because we try to compensate for what we feel is lacking by extending ourselves in other ways. For example, if you feel your social life is poor, you may compensate by doing other things—perhaps working late and on weekends. This might mask your loneliness, but it means your life revolves only around work, with no balancing factors, such as relaxing with family and friends.

• Get in touch with your inner self. By listening to your intuition you might discover how lonely you really feel; you can then make a choice about whether or not you want to do something about it.

• Be prepared to change. We often resist looking at how unbalanced we are because in order to regain our balance we need to change, which can be frightening. At first, it may be hard to adjust your entrenched behavior patterns, but it will come with practice.

love. This trait could be traced back to their mothers, who were themselves very needy and tended to smother their children. It is common for people to fall in love with those things in the other person that may repel them in the end. They find what they don't like about themselves in the other person.

For the next two years, Sam and Emma struggled to keep their relationship alive. They loved each other, but their life together was hell. Eventually, Sam suggested they see a couple counselor. She helped them to find a way to stop looking at what was going wrong in the other person and to discover what issues about dependence were causing problems for each of them individually. Both of them longed to be intimate but were afraid of being smothered.

This thing called love

The above story may not sound very romantic, but sharing your life with another human being soon reveals that the path of true love is not always as smooth as it is portrayed in the glossy world of advertising or romantic fiction. A partnership has to be strong, flexible, and resilient enough to survive not one blow, but many, over and over again. Each person must be able to withstand disappointment, irritation, and frustration—it's often when things go wrong that our love for another person is tested. People change and grow; jobs are lost or left; parents may become ill, children leave home—these are the everyday events that can put a great strain on the most loving relationships.

But while there needs to be room for anger and frustration to be openly expressed, in successful relationships love is always there as well. Relationships that don't work often fail because the negatives—the problems, failures, disappointments and complaints—outweigh the good things. Couples who stay together, however, spend more time making up and enjoying being with each other than they do feeling angry or hurt, usually because they make a great deal of effort to do this.

LOVE VS. NEED

It is sometimes difficult to see our relationships clearly because we find it impossible to separate love from need—the person we love is the person we need, and vice versa. Yet if we loved only the people we needed, then with the first frustration of that need we would stop loving them. This can occur temporarily in all relationships. Sally, for example, needed to see Paul as big and strong and responsible, and herself as weak and dependent. This in turn gave Paul that feeling of strength that he so needed.

A need for love

All intimate relationships are collusive to some extent because we love what we want to love in each other, and this is strongly influenced by need. Real, true love—the kind based on accepting a person as he or she really is—is less likely if you're very needy. The sort of collusion taking place in Paul and Sally's relationship will work until one or both of the partners decide they want to change, which will upset the "secret" pact unless the other person agrees to accept the change and change as well.

Love makes you strong

What happened, however, was that Paul became seriously ill. Despite herself, Sally felt anger, and then guilt because of this anger. "If I loved him I would care about him, not feel angry!" she thought. What was happening? Sally loved Paul deeply, but the Paul she loved was a strong, resilient male—not weak and dependent. Sally's anger was that he was "betraying" her by not being who she needed him to be; behind the anger there was fear that she had lost her only source of strength. But another part of Sally also felt that her behavior was unreasonable. She made an enormous effort to overcome her destructive feelings and to support Paul throughout his illness. Because the cycle of dependency had been broken, once Paul had recovered, their relationship continued to change and grow.

HAPPY FAMILIES

Family life is the foundation on which all our other experiences with human beings rest; it colors our subsequent relationships and expectations. Within the family, we practice not only our skills at assertiveness, socializing, sharing, giving, and taking, but we also learn firsthand about love. We discover what it means to hurt someone's feelings, to feel remorse and regret, to feel joy and pride—the gamut of emotions that inform human relations. More importantly, we learn the joy of sharing with people to whom we are close.

Families that offer an environment that is loving, secure, *and* flexible, one that enables each member to be him- or herself are the healthiest—and happiest—families. In such families, "home" isn't so much a physical place as the sense of security and safety that comes from having caring parents. Unfortunately, not all families are able to provide the necessary flexibility and support, which is when problems can occur, and individual members are damaged.

Safe as houses
A healthy, loving family provides all the security and safety we need.

There's no place like home

So what is the secret of the happy, healthy family? Studies have shown that there is no simple recipe for happiness, although certain important characteristics (described in the box, opposite) do emerge. In their book *Life and How to Survive It*, authors Robin Skynner and John Cleese discuss the results of research into healthy families in more detail. The picture they paint is rather unexpected and certainly not the conventional idea of a happy family. It appears that members of healthy families are very outgoing and have good relationships with people outside the family, as well as with each other. While they feel a great deal of affection for each other, they are also emotionally independent. Their love is not a possessive love—they don't need each other in a desperate way and are able to enjoy life fully when they are apart. Within the healthy family the parents are equal and united authority

figures. But this does not mean they are authoritarian, for they consult fully with their children and encourage them to voice their opinions. Ultimately, however, the children will respect the decision of the parents. Good communication is also vital, with everyone's views welcomed and respected. As a result, conflict is more readily and easily resolved. Another important characteristic of healthy families is a realistic and down-to-earth perception of the world, which enables members to handle situations and people appropriately. Finally, while many of us find change very unsettling and something to be avoided at all costs, the healthy family is good at dealing with change and even enjoys it.

When the bough breaks

At the opposite end of the spectrum is the unhealthy family, whose reasons for unhappiness are often the direct opposite of the factors defining the healthy family described above. Problems will occur, for example, if parents are possessive and try to control members of the family: Strong and possessive feelings are sometimes mistaken for love, but it is a love that relies on one party feeling that they have the right to invade the others' privacy and control their lives and feelings. When this is the case, other members of the family then feel unsure about their identity, confused as to their feelings, convinced of their worthlessness, unsure of their ability to function independently, and harbor a general mistrust of the world outside the family circle.

Most families, however, fall into a middle category. According to Skynner and Cleese, one of the most common failings of so-called average families is that the parents try too hard. They structure the family around firmly held principles, beliefs, and opinions, but as a result tend to be rigid and less able to enjoy life. These parents need to relax and love life more, and this *joie de vivre* will inevitably pervade the whole family.

TRAITS OF A HAPPY FAMILY

Parents have a strong relationship, are able to express their feelings, both positive and negative, and regularly make time for themselves.

The parents are consistently trustworthy and responsible in their dealings both toward each other and toward their children.

Each parent makes sure that he or she spends a certain amount of time alone with each child in shared activities.

The parents respect each other, and their children, as individuals, and behave accordingly, with consideration and courtesy.

The parents are demonstrative toward their children, who are consistently told and shown that they are loved and wanted.

Anger is allowed to be expressed freely and openly, within appropriate boundaries, and every effort is made to resolve problems.

Discipline, and clear, consistent boundaries, are firmly maintained with children, although the parents are not afraid to be flexible, too.

The privacy and solitude of both parents and children are respected and supported—there is room for each person to be who they are.

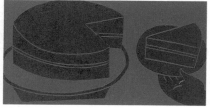

Sharing is actively encouraged between children, and parents and children, so that the rewards of giving can be experienced.

Family problems are shared and discussed openly. Older children are encouraged to get involved in decision-making.

The family is understood in terms of the world as a whole, and used to teach important issues outside the family.

Children are taught to be responsible by being gradually given more and more responsibility for themselves and others.

• Think about the different ways in which you could serve a greater community. Giving your time to a charity or voluntary organization is not the only way. You can bring pleasure to others through the arts, by teaching, or simply by being a responsible or supportive parent or citizen. Recognize, too, the ways in which you might be contributing already.

• Research potential opportunities for ways and areas in which you could apply your skills.

• Be clear about your responsibilities. In your anxiety to serve a cause, don't lose sight of your

A part of creation
You cannot shut out the world, so play your part in it positively.

more immediate obligations to your family, friends, and yourself. Any new responsibilities must fit in harmoniously with existing ones.

• Examine your motives: Make sure that you are not basing your decision on the opinions of others, or because of what you feel you "ought" to be doing. It will only be worthwhile if it is meaningful to you.

Making a difference

It is difficult to look beyond a generally accepted idea of what "serving the community" means, but it is important to understand service in much broader terms. Your contribution may involve some personal sacrifice, but equally it may not.

Your contribution to a worthy cause does not have to be on a grand scale for it to be worthwhile. Indeed, giving yourself to an individual usually requires greater humility, courage, and strength than becoming involved with a group or cause on a more dramatic scale in which your role is less personal. Whatever you decide to do, don't overwhelm yourself with feelings of inadequacy if you can give only in a limited way. It's more important to keep a positive focus on what you are doing in all the areas of your life in which you *are* playing your part. Your contribution, however small, is also a contribution to the greater scheme of things.

DEVELOP SELF-AWARENESS

To make sense of your own role within a larger community it's important to get a clear sense of who you are. This means examining your feelings and thoughts and striving to understand them, even when you do not like them very much. If you can come to accept who you are—both your strengths and weaknesses—you become stronger and more powerful. Unexpectedly, you will find that this exercise gives you a greater sense of how you fit into a broader picture, and have to depend, whether you like it or not, on others, as they depend on you.

Without a strong sense of self-awareness your ability to respond is limited. You are less able to cope with change or act as you would like in difficult situations—you may lose your temper, or panic unduly, for example. You are unable to give an honest response to a given situation because you are confused. Many different emotions—fear of the unknown, depression in the face of a desperate situation, shame that you are not doing enough to help—make straightforward reasoning almost impossible. But all these emotions can be made more manageable if you have first established a strong sense of self.

THE HUMAN TOUCH

We may think that we can survive without human contact, but in reality it would be very hard to achieve. As the French historian Jules Michelet said, "Life is set ablaze by and galvanized by life: this light extinguishes in isolation. The more life interacts with the lives of others, the more it can become one with them, gaining strength, happiness, and richness." Humans are by nature "sociable" animals, instinctively seeking out the company of others. The need for mutual support, and a sense of belonging and "connectedness," is, for the majority of us, one of life's great driving forces.

Insular or sociable?

Few of us are truly capable of finding a solitary life fulfilling. We need others around us, but for some people this is very hard to achieve. They have great difficulty being at ease with others, and prefer to retreat into splendid isolation where there is no danger of getting hurt. Whether you think of yourself as a loner or as someone who likes to be in the thick of things will depend on how you perceive yourself and your place in the world around you. This, in turn, will be determined mainly by your early experiences of life as an individual and as a member of a group—whether the group was your family, your class, your sports team, or your friends. In particular, it is through your family, both immediate and extended, that you first learn about other people and how to react or not react to make your own needs felt. You learn what is and what is not acceptable behavior—the nuts and bolts of human interaction—from your parents, guardians, siblings, and friends.

Family influences

How your parents interacted with the outside world will almost certainly have influenced your own behavior. Some families are outgoing: they get involved in their community, have a busy social life, and a wide circle of friends. Others prefer to close ranks and keep the family circle limited to just the immediate members and a few close friends—behavior that is often based on a deep mistrust and discomfort of the outside world. If your family is like the latter you may have absorbed their suspicion toward "outsiders." Anything different or unusual would have been either considered threatening or viewed with wariness. As a child you would have received this message and as an adult you may still feel the same way—that only people who are like you are safe. This self-imposed isolation can curb curiosity and reduce interest in anything new or unusual, particularly other people. If, on the other hand, your family was outgoing and had an active interchange with the outside world, which they introduced to you as friendly, interesting, and non-threatening, then you are more likely to seek and enjoy friendships and build rewarding relationships within your community and working life.

An open-and-shut case
If you prefer to keep to yourself, closing the door on the unfamiliar and unknown, you are cutting yourself off not only from all that is painful about human interaction, but all that is joyful and rich, too. The antidote is to seek to involve people in your life, and actively welcome them.

Taking a risk

Human interactions are trade-offs. By getting involved with others, either socially, at home, at work, or within the community, and getting involved in what all these people are doing, you are both giving and receiving. No matter how isolated you may feel, it *is* possible to get closer to others, although you will have to be prepared to take a risk and do things differently from how you have done them before. If you can start to identify with the needs and problems of others, you are more likely to have your own needs met. This happens through helping others, and therefore helping yourself by fulfilling your need to be involved and valued by others. This may seem a daunting prospect—but just think how great the potential rewards are.

GIVE TO GET

Showing concern for others is one of the most satisfying aspects of human interaction, yet it is not something that can be taught; it has to come from inside you. True concern has its roots in self-concern and empathy with others—the ability to put yourself in another person's shoes. And we all possess these qualities, if we dig deep enough. Caring for others is a talent we all have, but it may have become hidden under a self-protective layer of not getting involved.

Sometimes, if you are in need yourself, you may find it difficult to be concerned about others; how can you give what you yourself don't have? However, if you ask for help—and then receive it—you will find that you are able to "top up" your supplies of love and caring so that you have enough to give to others.

Bonding with nature
The empathy humans and dolphins share can be harnessed and used in therapeutic treatments.

Art therapy:

Every child knows the satisfaction of putting pen to paper, and children often use drawing to express ideas about themselves and others that they cannot yet put into words. It is equally effective for adults, helping them explore many issues—especially those that are unconscious. Art therapy is now well established as a therapeutic tool in schools and hospitals. Art can help us to get in touch with another side of ourselves, to explore what is hidden to us and give it expression. There are many workshops that use art to help people on their inner journey.

Voice workshops:

The idea behind singing and chanting techniques is that releasing the voice also helps to release many painful emotions. Through singing and chanting, either on your own or in a group, you can become more in tune with your body. This process can be healing, energizing, relaxing, and uplifting. Some voice therapists teach sonic massage, in which the different vibrations produced by chanting are used to massage invisible energy centers in the body known as *chakras*.

Into the New Age

As the interest in "alternative" therapies grows, perhaps in reaction to the increasingly frenzied pace of this technological age, the range is becoming ever more diverse, from crystal therapy and rebirthing, to color therapy and astrology. Here is a taste of just two such therapies:

Swimming with dolphins: The fascination with dolphins perhaps lies in the fact that these attractive creatures live in harmony with their environment and display an affinity toward man. Dolphins appear to touch people very deeply, communicating a *joie de vivre* that "speaks" to people. Numerous workshops offer supervised contact with dolphins. Dolphin fans attest to their powers of healing—in Australia, for example, severely handicapped children have responded to the animals where other methods have failed to elicit a reaction.

Dreamwork: No one really knows why we dream, but dreams may be about working out things that happened in the past, working to solve current problems, and, some believe, forecasting the future. Dreams are thought to be the unconscious part of ourselves trying to communicate with the conscious. Dream analysis is a fascinating subject, and there are individual therapists and workshops that specialize in this area. There are numerous books on dream interpretation, but it is often easy to work out yourself what is going on in your mind. As soon as you wake up, write down your dreams. You may well find a pattern emerging that you can, for example, link to recent or forthcoming events in your life that have troubled or excited you.

How Reflective Are You?

Think of an average day in your life. Are there any moments of quiet reflection during which you simply enjoy some stillness or think about where you and your life are going? Chances are that you are so caught up in a dizzy round of working, sleeping, eating, shopping, cooking, fixing the car, that the idea of taking time out not to *do*, but to *think,* seems impossible. And yet, however busy you are, it is easy—and essential for your future happiness—for you to snatch some reflective moments in one way or another.

Keeping your dreams alive

Whether you take a few minutes to daydream as you stare out of a train window, or are able to find the time to spend a weekend away at a retreat to be alone with your thoughts, such periods of quiet reflection bring a number of benefits:

• Breathing space

Reflective moments relax and refresh you mentally by giving you a break from your routine. Mental well-being normally means physical well-being, too. The need for some solitude is understood in all walks of life, all over the world. A time for reflection gives us the calming solitude that is important for everyone. When you sit alone and watch raindrops chasing each other down a window pane, or get lost in old memories as you lie in a warm bath, you are giving your mind a valuable rest, thereby helping you to recharge your batteries. No matter how busy you are, make a point of taking a few minutes out from time to time; remember, it's not always the length of the break that is important, but the break itself.

• Relief from pressure

Daydreaming gives you a chance to chew ideas over without any pressure. Some of the insights you come up with today might be useful tomorrow, or ten years from now, but you can be sure that they will never be wasted. Your times of relaxed reflection, as your mind ponders matters great and small, are the rare times that you are using your mental powers in a completely open and free way. There is no pressure to come up with the right answer to a problem, or indeed any answers at all. The term "daydreaming" is extremely apt because, just as your brain sorts all kinds of information while you sleep, so when you mentally switch off and daydream, you are actually sifting calmly through a wealth of ideas, impressions, and sensations, although you are probably unaware that you are doing so.

When you are relaxed, your brainwaves slow down and you are literally in a more accepting frame of mind. All kinds of creative ideas can come out of this unstructured, free-ranging mental activity: Einstein, for example, was struck by his theory of relativity as he gazed at sunbeams one sunny day.

• A sense of identity

Our lives today are so busy, full of pressures both important and trivial, that it is more important than ever to have quiet moments where only you and your musings exist. This is your opportunity to get to know yourself better. Maintaining a strong sense of your identity—your talents and faults, hopes and fears—is vital if you are to find happiness and fulfillment, but this can only be nurtured in time by yourself. It is only in moments alone that you will find the space for the real, natural you to emerge. Once you have a definite feel for the issues that truly concern you, you can decide which goals you want to work toward, aims that will also consolidate your identity. Then, you can plan the steps you want to take in the future.

LEARN TO CONCENTRATE

Look closely at a child staring into a rock pool, or eyeing a fly as it crawls across a pane of glass, and you will learn all that you need to know about constructive reflection. A child is totally absorbed, yet relaxed; accepting, yet alive to the moment. This is a talent that we tend to lose as we get older and our lives become cluttered. We constantly try to do two things at once, watching TV as we eat, talking as we scan a book. As a result we prefer our information, even our experiences, in small, manageable chunks, and gradually become less able to concentrate for long periods of time.

Make time to dream
Daydreaming gives your brain the space and freedom to explore ideas and impressions in a creative way.

But can these be quality experiences without the time to reflect on them? In his book *The Art of Being*, Erich Fromm advocates the value of concentration, and describes how to learn it. Be completely still for ten minutes, and try to be aware only of what is going on inside you. At first, other thoughts will filter through and you will feel uncomfortable, even sleepy, but practice will help you overcome this. You can then choose an item, thought, or feeling to focus on. Remember, you cannot force concentration or the thoughts will not come freely.

A new approach

Donald's problems, however, were very different. He was an extremely successful, self-made businessman with a happy family life. But whenever the subject of education came up, he felt very uncomfortable. He had disliked school, leaving early and without any qualifications. Despite his evident success as an adult, Donald doubted his intellectual capacity.

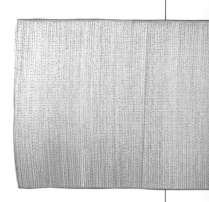

One day, a few weeks before Donald and his family were to go on vacation to Italy, Donald's wife bought herself some foreign-language videos. They involved new learning techniques, playlets, songs, and jokes to make learning fun. Donald overheard his wife listening to them one day and was astonished to find that he was learning the language with ease. Now that he could see a point to what he was doing, and he was being offered a congenial way of assimilating new information, he began to enjoy the learning process. On his return from holiday, he found that he wanted to seek out more such opportunities, and enrolled in French classes.

Taking minor risks is an unavoidable part of living more courageously, because the only way you will change your life is to do things differently, and this can be uncomfortable at first. If you do what you've always done, you'll get what you've always got. But if you try something you've *never* done before, who knows where it may lead you?

Steps to success
To live life to the full involves taking calculated risks—with each small, but challenging step, you will gain the confidence to move on to greater achievements.

RISKY BUSINESS?

Everyone will have different ideas about what it means to take a small risk—introducing yourself to a stranger at a party may be your idea of extending your comfort zone, whereas for someone else, learning to swim as an adult offers a considerable challenge. Here are some risks that you might like to consider taking. Some of them you may do already—and find easy—others may sound terribly difficult. Decide which risk you are going to take, either from the list below or one of your own choice. Once you've completed the task, take another! The only proviso, of course, is that the risks you take should not upset anyone else.

• Cook a dish you find difficult to prepare
• Ask someone out on a date
• Confront someone who has wronged you
• Tell your partner a secret
• Speak out for what you believe in
• Talk to a stranger
• Join a social club
• Try a new restaurant
• Apply for a new job
• Learn to dance
• Help a neighbor
• Change your hair-style
• Wear an outfit that gives you a new, different look
• Travel to a part of the world you've never visited before
• Learn a new sport
• Take night classes
• Learn a foreign language
• Go and see a film or play you wouldn't normally choose
• Give some of your spare time to a charity

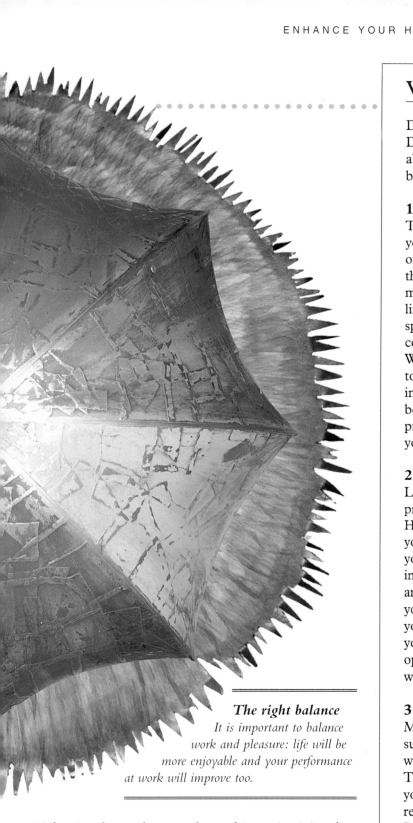

The right balance
It is important to balance work and pleasure: life will be more enjoyable and your performance at work will improve too.

Mike is clear about where his priorities lie. Sometimes he finds it difficult to juggle work and home, but he never loses sight of his need to do well at his job, and his need to enjoy a family life. None of us are that different from Mike. We all have pressures to contend with, but we can all find a way to accommodate work and play.

WHAT'S TO STOP YOU?

Do you feel unable to enjoy your leisure time? Described below, with advice on what to do about it, are the three main reasons why you may be having this problem:

1. Lack of time

The daily demands of life are such that unless you deliberately make the effort to include some of the things you like in your activities, most of them may be edged out. But do you really manage your time efficiently? Everyone has some limitations placed upon them, but most of us spend far too much time on perhaps the most common leisure activity—watching television. While there is much enjoyment and stimulation to be gained from watching TV, it is easy to get into a habit of watching anything that happens to be on. Become a selective viewer and watch only programs you specifically want to see; in this way you'll free up your time for many other activities.

2. Lack of money

Lack of money can be a major factor in preventing you from doing what you want. However, there are often ways of adapting what you would like to do into something cheaper. If you can't afford to visit that new Thai restaurant in town, why not have fun buying a cookbook and investigating all the different ingredients you'd need to cook a Thai meal for yourself. Or if you'd love to take a vacation but do not see how you could afford it, investigate other cheaper options such as camping, house-swapping, and working holidays.

3. Lack of support

Many people feel guilt or experience a lack of support from their partner, friends, or children when they want to spend time on themselves. There are two alternatives: either you involve your family in what you want to do, or you remain assertive and stick to what you want. Relationships, friendship, and family life are about a balance of what you want and what others want. Ultimately, if you are happy in all aspects of your life, then those around you will benefit from it, too.

BACK TO NATURE

Many people realize intuitively that the natural world can have an important part to play in their lives, and can lift their spirits when they are feeling down. Just think about how good it makes you feel going out to work on a bright, crisp morning rather than a dull, gray one. Being immersed in nature can increase the positive feelings you have about the world by heightening your spiritual connection, the realization that you are a small part of a greater whole, and—in times of stress or trouble—making you feel life is worth living again.

Cultivate your garden

What can you do to feel more connected to nature? First of all, there is no need to move to the country in order to spend more time with nature. Most towns and cities have green areas, and we are often slow to appreciate what we have on our doorsteps. Gardening, for example, is a very popular leisure activity, which involves contact with nature, physical exercise, and creativity.

Rolling up your sleeves, getting your hands into the soil, and watching your plants grow is immensely satisfying. Enjoying gardening does not necessarily mean having a garden, but doing any sort of cultivation—from maintaining a large yard to caring for indoor pot plants. If you don't have a garden yourself, most people who live in apartments are able to grow flowers, small shrubs, and herbs in window boxes. If you are a novice, there are many books that can teach you how to create magnificent displays from a variety of pots.

You can also bring a sense of the country into your apartment with arrangements of cut flowers or branches coming into bud; for more permanent displays, use houseplants to reflect the changing seasons: hyacinths in spring, miniature roses in summer, and something exotic like amaryllis in winter.

Natural beauty

The beauty of the natural world isn't confined to living, growing things, of course. One of the pleasures of visiting a beach, for example, is collecting pebbles and shells; at home, put them in bowls that you can dip your hand into as you pass by, or display fine specimens separately. You could also make a feature of driftwood or lichen-covered branches—use your creativity to draw in all those natural elements that give you pleasure, and serve as a reminder of a world faraway from the city.

Urban oases
There are many ways to bring nature into your life, even when you live in the heart of the city.

OUT AND ABOUT

Here are some ideas of how to become closer to nature that can be incorporated into your life easily:

• Many cities and towns have walking or cycling groups that organize trips to local beauty spots or interesting places inaccessible to the general public.

• Most towns of any size have large parks, some of which are so big that you can forget you are in a built-up area. Try and spend some time in them.

• Next time you are able to take a short break, try a weekend in the country. Choose somewhere off the beaten track, and different from your daily milieu.

• Some people feel particularly calm and peaceful when they are close to water—so visit a lake in a park, the ocean, or even a large outdoor pool.

• If you like sport, combine physical challenge with natural beauty by trying mountain climbing, sailing, hill-walking, or a similar outdoor activity.

• Help conserve the natural world by joining one of the many environmental groups. Some preservation, wildlife, or nature groups may offer holidays where you pay minimum board or lodgings in return for conservation work.